CLAWS IN MY CLEAVAGE!

Poems of Life, Love, and Other Calamities

JENNY CONNER KEELEY

© 2018

All poems are original and copyrighted works of Jenny Conner Keeley

1

DEDICATION

Dedicated to my family, Military, all First Responders, and Victim Advocates; especially the 9/11 NOVA teams, and my Brothers and Sisters in Blue at Heath PD, Ohio. We all surely share the same demented humor, the same moments of madness...and have shed the same private tears... BE SAFE and remember it's laughter that keeps us from going crazy!

With great love,

Jenny

(Detective Jenny Keeley, Heath PD, Ohio '74-'94)

'CLAWS IN MY CLEAVAGE'

Claws in my cleavage, paws in my hair,

Claws kneading my pillow,

CLAWS EVERYWHERE!!

I looked at the clock, 'twas a quarter to five,

I can't move my legs, I'm barely alive!

The kitty is purring; I've not heard such a noise.

There's no reprieve! Now she's playing with toys!

Lola jumps and she throws, I think I'm in hell,

Cause the toy that she's chosen
IS THE ONE WITH THE BELL!!!

She tosses and leaps, husband snores like a log.

But his reverie is short...

Lola has awakened the dog!

Emmy jumps to her feet, her claws all a clatter.

I said, "NO! STAY DOWN!!"

...but it didn't matter.

75 pounds of pup jumped up on our bed,

Clawed over my back,

she didn't care that I bled.

The chase was on; it was time for play,

Dog and cat in our bed... and it wasn't yet day!

But then came a roar as Poppa Bear arose.

"GOOD GAWD! WHAT'S GOING ON?!"

was the question he posed.

His bellowing voice caused both girls to run.

The party was over,
the dancing was done.

Claws in my cleavage, paws in my hair,

Claws kneading my pillow,

CLAWS EVERYWHERE!!

###

(Dedicated to everyone who sleeps with their pets!)

(To Daddy with Love;

John R. Conner, US Naval Aviator WWII)

'I CAN FLY'

When I was just a young child

gazing up at studded skies,

A comet streaked through liquid clouds

splashing Stardust in my eyes.

In those magic moments

of the Twilight and the still,

My heart beat as a Pilot's heart

...I know it always will.

Now I soar and race with Eagles

...fly Sea to shining Sea.

I've barrel-rolled through blazing skies

...and found the best in me.

Red-tail Hawks have stretched beside me

Catching thermals on the rise...

Challenging my fixed-wing craft

as they ballet through the skies.

I sought and chased the Angels

till I lost them in the Light,

Mirrored in my silver wings

...more blinding than the night.

When my time on Earth is over

and my Soul looks to the Sky,

Rejoice as feathered wings lift me...

"I can fly; I can fly...**I CAN FLY!!**"

###

'WHERE DOLPHINS FLY'

Mother Earth does sing to me

    with birds in breathless harmony.

As evening embers fade to violet sky,

    In purple grace...the Dolphins fly!!

Waves the color of emerald eyes,

    roll as languid summer sighs;

rise and fall to sea gulls' cries

    ...eternal as Love that never dies.

    ###

'KAYAKER'S PRAYER'

This Prayer is whispered to the God

of Water... and the Wind.

We'll not disturb your Creatures

who wait around each bend.

A sentry Stork stands shore guard,

an Eagle takes a bough.
A Manatee rolls lazily,

a Whale sings to his cow!

Confines of Earth are broken

upon this watery way.

Each paddle stroke propels me

in perfect freedom on this day.

I ask for strength to power

this ancient craft to Sea.

To fight the Surf and crashing Waves

...TO FIND THE BEST IN ME!

Gliding on Tides of darkness

with Moonlight in my wake,

I'll follow shining Viking Stars

on whatever course they take.

I make this Kayaker's Promise

...This you can believe.

"ALL I'LL TAKE ARE MEMORIES

...WAKE IS ALL I'LL LEAVE."

In these magic moments

came a mystical surprise.

While paddling, I saw God, today

...In a Dolphin's eyes!!

###

'WICKED CHOCOLATE'

Chocolate...wicked Chocolate...

Such a hold you have on me!

Alluring in my waking hours...

haunting my Dreams to be.

Chocolate...wicked Chocolate,

your heart is surely cold.

Please, loosen your addictive grip

and release your luscious hold.

Chocolate...wicked Chocolate...

you taste of Paradise!

I listened to your Siren's Song

and fell for Cocoa lies.

Chocolate...wicked Chocolate...

I'm growing to despise

your silky, smooth deliciousness

'CAUSE I BLAME YOU FOR MY THIGHS!!

10

'WE WILL DEFEND'

Without being 'politically correct'

I intend to have my say.

I believe in 'One Nation under God'

and I love the U.S.A.

The Second Amendment guarantees

Our Right to keep and bear arms,

To protect our lives and families

and America, from harm.

So, do not try to take our guns,

the Constitution, we will defend.

Do not try to infringe our Rights.

We will fight until the end.

Our borders need to be secure

from all who would invade.

Illegal means…'against the Law',

and lawbreakers should be afraid.

Bring our soldiers home from foreign lands

to serve on American soil.

Stop the taxing and spending madness

…mine our own gas, wind and oil.

Washington has spiraled out of control,

the politicians can go to Hell.

So, pay very close attention

…and listen for the 'Liberty Bell'!

###

'BLUE TEARS' (7/8/'16)

There's blood on the streets in Dallas.

    Blue tears are falling like rain.

Explanations and answers elude us.

    We're lost in the anguish of pain.

We know that all lives matter,

    but they don't seem to matter to all.

Each stop turns to confrontation.

    Every day a Policeman falls.

We looked to Obama for wisdom;

    for words to ease our grief.

We hear the same empty rhetoric

    ...we're left with no lasting relief.

The media rushes to judgement;

       without basis of trial, to indict.

Due process is denied to Policemen.

       Race mongers seek to incite.

There's blood on the streets in Dallas,

       Five dead and seven critical remain.

Hold your Brothers and Sisters dearly.

       Blue tears are falling like rain.

       ###

'VOW TO A FALLEN OFFICER'

A Policeman will be carried today,

    passing lines of suits of Blue.

We'll all salute as he's buried.

    We'll each die a little, too.

The Stars and Stripes fly at half mast,

    bagpipes are playing lowly.

Mourners brace at attention

    ...the Honor Guard passes slowly.

Today we stand together

    with faces set and grim,

for he was one of us

    ...and we were part of him.

As helpless tears roll down our cheeks

it seems there's nothing we can do!

But there is a vow that we can make,

and swear it, solemnly... to you.

For one brief moment, your torch was down,

till another Cop lifted the flame.

The fire flickered, caught and burned anew

when the Angels called your name.

You did not go gently into the Night,

and died an honorable death.

Just know, we will continue the Fight

...as long as one of us draws breath.

###

(Written after attending the funeral of Lancaster PD, OH
Officer Brett Markwood; murdered in the line of duty,
2/21/1993.)

'GOLFER'S LAMENT'

I looked at the clock…'twas a quarter of five;

I can't feel my legs, I'm barely alive.

The golf course is calling…too strong to ignore.

I dress in the dark as I'm crossing the floor.

But the rattling of clubs as I was leaving the house

Broke the sleepy silence…and awakened my spouse!

"WHERE ARE YOU GOING?

THERE ARE CHORES TO BE DONE!"

"PAINTING AND MOWING…THERE'S NO TIME FOR FUN!!"

"I'LL BE BACK BY TWO!" I ran for the door…

When she heaved the vase, all I heard was FORE!"

I woke in the driveway, the scene was a blur!

She didn't miss me…

BUT I'M GONNA MISS HER!!!

###

'HUNTING DREAMS'

Come hunt 'The Red Buffalo'

    in the Kansas of coyote calls.

Track trophy Bucks through black-jacks,

    Stargaze at Butcher Falls.

Flush Turkey from the Tallgrass;

    fish from the pristine lake.

See Red-tail Hawks stand sentry

    ...Beware the Rattlesnake!

Moonlit Buffalo graze the Bluestem

    as 'Prairiehenge' casts its spell.

Watch Eagles riding thermals

    ...hear a distant Wildcat yell.

Experience 'The Red Buffalo'

    under skies of crystal blue,

in the Flint Hills of Chautauqua County

    ...where hunting dreams come true!

###

'POOR LITTLE HENRY'

Poor little Henry...

    Such a beautiful child

With mischievous blue eyes

    and blonde curls, free and wild!

He's trying hard to use a fork

    but seems to miss his mouth.

Food is dropping in his lap

    ...his napkin has gone south!

"SIT UP...SIT DOWN..."

    Bandage on your 'ouch'.

Momma's going to 'pop' you

    If you talk or if you slouch!

Poor little Henry,

    syrup on his clothes,

butter smeared across his face

    ...a booger in his nose!

"STOP IT, HENRY! QUIT! DON'T DO IT!!"

His Mom was about to blow.

His sisters are back from the 'ladies room',

Now Henry has to go!!

Momma has lost her patience,

The girls all seem so fine,

But Henry has ired his Momma,

poor boy has crossed her line.

"BEHAVE! BEHAVE! BEHAVE!!!"

Momma has lost her cool.

"I'M GOING TO BEAT YOUR #@&# BUTT!!"

She seems a little cruel.

Poor little Henry,

try not to laugh too loud,

'cause I'm going to trip your Momma

...when she passes in the crowd!!

###

'SURFER'S PRAYER'

"This Prayer is issued to Ku'emanu

and Neptune's briny ears...

Let me surf forever amped and stoked

...always facing my finest fears."

"Let me smack the lip of massive bombs

riding curls of azure blue.

Protect me from sharks and impact zones

with my fins underfoot... and true."

"When gnarly waves engulf me

as cliffs rising from the Sea,

Let me ride this board to Freedom

...and find the 'mana' in me."

"Protect me from hairy coral heads.

　　In soaring aerials...let me fly!

Let the fetch and swells amaze me

　　...let me 'surf out' before I die."

When my surfing days are over,

　　my final wish will be...

"Paddle my ashes past the breakers

　　...and return me to the Sea."

　　　###

'CLUB LADIES'

We are the Golf Club Ladies...

it is an honored name.

We're proud of all the many skills

We've learned to play this game.

Kindred spirits with Mother Nature

...because she's a Lady too,

we enjoy the beauty of her Great Outdoors

on Greens under skies of blue.

Starting to play this addictive game

...we didn't know a thing.

We didn't know a Slice from a Hook

...or how to grip a Ping!

We learned how to drive after Teeing off

...and Putting was really tough.

The only thing that was easy to learn

...WAS HOW TO LAND IN THE ROUGH!!!

We love to race our Golf Carts

    ... on Cart Paths, where allowed,

illegally cutting through Fairways

    at speeds making Danica proud!!

Club Ladies have an advantage

    over Golfers who are male.

We can wash our Balls in public

    ...AND NOBODY GOES TO JAIL!!!!

When our Game is over,

    just watch our Golf Carts roll!

If anyone wants to catch us

    ...WE'LL BE AT THE 19TH HOLE!!!

###

'FIRST FISH JOY'

I remember all those years ago

    ...fishing from the bank,

when a Catfish took my night crawler

    and gave my line a yank!

I remember how I set the hook

    with a flick of a bamboo pole,

then felt the jerk of a fighting fish

    as I fought him to the shoal.

Within the man that lives today

    beats the heart of that little boy,

and when fishing, I still feel the thrill

    of that youngster's 'first fish' joy!

I've fished the turquoise Caribbean;

the Atlantic and Pacific, too.

Done rivers wild and mountain streams

...all vivid shades of blue.

I've traveled far to distant Seas

...to exotic ports of call.

I've fished for every kind of fish

...and almost caught them all!

But none have made the memories

...no matter the size or take,

as that first, exciting Channel Cat

caught from the bank

of my hometown lake.

###

'COLONOSCOPY BLUES'

Drink this, they said, but they didn't reveal

    the names of the witches who concocted with zeal!

BOIL...BOIL...CAULDRON BUBBLE!!!

    The foaming elixir soon had me in trouble!

There was fire and wind! There was smoke and flames!

    I spoke in voices...and called my Doctor names!

Dracula's spawn in scrubs sidled up to my bed.

    "I need your hand," is all I remember she said.

My Doctor arrived, I was drugged and gowned

    Then poked and probed...then turned upside down!

When the concoction hit, the emissions were randy,

    I thought I was fat, turns out...I was sandy!!!

The rest of the day seemed to go quite well,

      But the following night was a descent into Hell!

Fevers and chills...shivering and shaking,

      Temperature soaring...no sense was I making.

"Go to the E.R.", the nurse line avowed.

      "Sounds like an infection...better go now."

Then the Doctor called and prescribed some pills.

If infection doesn't kill me... rancid medicine will!!

No pain, no hurt, it doesn't seem right.

      Temperature's climbing...I'm up all night.

So, this is the saga of the search for clues

Of the source of the misery of my colonoscopy blues!!!

      ###

'EARLY BIRD LAMENT'

I am the 'Early Bird'

...with eyes of 'bloodshot' red.

I always get that dirty worm

'cause I'm the first one out of bed.

This morning's alarm 'twas a quarter of three,

I can't feel my face...I'm not sure if it's me!

Sleep deprivation is not worth the price.

I'm most often grumpy...and never look nice!

My nails are a mess.

My hair is awry!

There's mud in my cleavage

...and a bug in my eye!

The damned worms are gross

 ...they wrap 'round my beak.

They're hard to swallow

...and get stuck in my cheek!

As if life wasn't hard enough

 ...or my options thinner,

I just checked the paper

      ...I'm on the menu for DINNER!!

       ###

'FLYING LOW TO YOU'

I'm landing in Fort Lauderdale
as a Fly girl on JetBlue.
Then I'm driving 80 on 95
...flying low to you.

Seattle's Northern Lights were dancing
in every imaginable hue.
The Las Vegas moon was waxing
...Denver's Rockies dressed in blue.

New York's skyline was spectacular
...Lady Liberty waved her light!
Miami's nightscape sparkled in greeting
...Boston's lobster was pure delight!

Made the LaGuardia turn this morning;
then back to Lauderdale town.
The Olds was waiting in the parking lot
for me to put the pedal down!

I took off my scarf
and kicked off my heels,

I've got wings on my sweater

...and wings on my wheels!

Michael Buble' sings on the radio

how he "never more will roam."

His plaintive words tear at my heart

...I too, just want to go home.

A little house in a coastal town

beckons me home, tonight.

Four hours north by interstate

...twisting silver by full moonlight.

This Olds 98 on 95

is roaring towards 44.

Home is where my true love waits

...behind a beveled glass door.

Now, I'm driving 80 on 95

...flying low to you.

Winged wheels lifting over the road

...I'm flying home to you.

###

'OLD BROADS'

Once we were beauties...or so it's been said.

Our hair fell in curls...our Lips pouted red.

Our eyes were a shimmer. They glistened and shined.

Our figures were svelte...we had little 'behinds'.

Our skin was unblemished, nary a wrinkle or fold,

our posture...erect! Our bosoms were bold!

Now bunions are growing...we keep losing things.

We're growing mustaches...our arms flap like wings!

So, let's drink till we're stupid, celebrate till we're blue.

If we wake in the morning... we'll sober up with a Brew!

###

'NURSES'

Nurses come from Heaven;

    each on a special day.

They keep their angelic kindness...

    but lose their wings along the way.

These Angels walk among us

    wearing scrubs and stethoscopes.

They offer comfort to our families

    and bolster healing hopes.

When doctors are too distant

    ...or too busy to explain,

Nurses will allay our fears

    and listen to our pain.

When darkness falls around us

in unfamiliar night,

An Angel comes into our room

to hold our hand until the light.

Angels walk among us,

gliding through sterile halls,

giving smiles and a gentle touch

to answer frightened calls.

We send this prayer to Heaven,

thanking Angels for their care,

and to let them know we appreciate

the Nurses that they share.

###

'MIGHTY DUNHAM' (1927-2016)

85 years it had been his dream

...to hit a 'Hole in One'.

He had no clue this was the Monday

...that he'd finally get it done!!

A large mound blocked the distant green

of #12's downhill...par three.

A hush fell over the usual crowd

...Mighty Dunham was at the tee!

He pulled out his trusted Calloway

...did a quick scan of the sky.

Then swung with the strength of destiny

...and let that Crystal fly!!!!

That golden ball just sprouted wings;

heading straight for #12's pin.

It flew One Hundred and Sixty yards;

It hit…it bounced…**IT ROLLED IN!!!!**

At first he couldn't believe his eyes;

then his friends began to cheer!

He jumped up in excitement

…AND ALMOST SPILLED HIS BEER!!!!

Ormonds's beautiful Riverbend Golf Club

is now an historic place.

November 12th, 2012,

DUNHAM DOMINGUS HIT AN ACE!!!!!!

(Rest in peace, Dunham. We miss you…SWING ON!!)

'THE INDIAN RIVER BLUES'

Hum a tune of Mosquito Lagoon

    Kick off both your shoes.

Dance the way the palm trees sway

    to the Indian River Blues.

Calls of Whales in the distance,

    cries of Dolphins so near.

Songs of the surf compel me

    ...to hold New Smyrna, dear.

Pirates of Ponce Inlet

    buried treasures without clues.

From their wat'ry graves you'll hear them

    singin' the Indian River Blues.

When the full moon rises

    In purple skies sublime,

Pull your Lover close to you

    ...and begin to sway in time.

So, dosey-do right and aleman left,

      you have only your heart to lose.

Open your arms in a sweeping bow

      singin' the Indian River Blues.

Follow the lead of the Pelican;

      two step, dip and spin.

Hold your Lover cheek to cheek

      and dance till the tide comes in!

So, hum a tune of Mosquito Lagoon,

      kick off both your shoes.

Dance the way the palm trees sway

      ...to the Indian River Blues.

###

'I AM A POLICEMAN'

I am a Policeman
...and proud I'll always be.
'To Protect and Serve'...my motto,
    you are safe because of me.

You'll hear our wailing sirens
...see our lights of flashing blue;
but you'll never know the things we see
    ...or do the things we do.

I am a Policeman;
but a smile's a thin disguise.
If you really want to know me
    ...look into my eyes.

We see life's inhumanity,
at least, that's what it seems.
Some things, I wish, could be unseen
    ...awake...or in my dreams.

Give blessings for the guardians
who patrol both day and night,
who risk their lives in that thin blue line
    ...and often times...lose the fight.

I am a Policeman
...and proud I'll always be.
'To Protect and Serve'...my motto
    ...you are safe because of me.

· ###

'A LIPLOCK WITH A GLASS OF GIN'

One night he decided to do the town

    and proceeded to pay his dues.

He scrubbed, cologned, and cinched his belt

    through the loops of his denim blues.

He washed and rinsed and combed his hair

    at least those he could save.

Those remaining hairs are true Marines,

    The few, the Proud...the Brave!

Never had there ever been such a man...

    black T-shirt and a Harley hat.

He biked to the bar and strode inside

    ...Mighty Jones was at the bat!

He saw her across the smoky room;

    all young, and blonde, and thin.

She smiled that smile, you know the one,

        while in a lip lock with a glass of gin.

She was the stuff of desires and dreams

        all long-limbed and luscious curves.

Her face would make a grown man cry,

        Her body turned good men to pervs!

Their eyes locked in a star-crossed gaze,

        She started a slow-dance with him.

He threw back a beer, his intentions clear

        ...his smile and her hips in rhythm.

He blew out his chest and sucked in his gut,

        sure she'd never have eyes for another.

She leaned in to say, words he regrets to this day...

"Hey...you went to school with my Mother!!"

###

'MOTHER MOUNTAIN'

Mother Mountain speaks to me

     with birds in four-part harmony.

The morning light awakes the Lark

     ...Whippoorwills retreat into the dark.

Under watercolors of pink and grey

     a Sparrow sings in place.

The misted morning turns to day

     ...a Bullfrog lends his bass.

The majesty of these ancient skies

     stirs deep memories in me,

As ancestors gaze now through my eyes

     ...at their beautiful Tennessee.

###

'BABY BLOOMERS'

Walking down a country road

    I found to my surprise,

A field of Baby Bloomers

    ...with dancing, joyful eyes!

So many blooms to choose from;

    Petunias, Magnolias...a Rose.

Sunflowers, Begonias, Hibiscus

    ...carefully, I chose.

Gently, I picked the stem

    and carried home my prize,

To share with friends and family

    ...this Lily with sapphire eyes!!

    ###

(For our darling granddaughter, Lily)

'THE ANGELS LET KENNA STAY'

Makenna Renee came from Heaven

on a very special day.

She kept her cherubic dimples,

but lost her wings along the way.

She cuddled into her Daddy's arms

where she was safe and warm.

Entering our lives like sunshine

...but taking our hearts by storm!

Kenna laughs and talks with Angels

...though we can't see them, there.

They guard and watch her sleeping

...casting moonbeams in her hair.

We thought we knew what joy was

...Until that precious day

When Love took the form of our granddaughter

...and the Angels let Kenna stay!

###

'THE OLD MAN'

The old man sat at the table,

the table of his hosts,

and began to tell them stories

of ghouls, goblins, and ghosts!

The children sat at attention,

as rapt as rapt could be,

listening to his horrid tales

...of intriguing mystery.

"Ghosts are all around, he said

...in the walls and under the floor.

They're all just waiting to GET you

...THERE'S ONE... BY THE DOOR!!!"

The children spun to see the ghost.

The old man extinguished the light.

Children ran screaming in all directions

...grabbed by fingers of night!!

But then a candle flickered,

casting a glow on the old man's beard.

"There's no such thing as ghosts," he said,

and while laughing...

HE DISAPPEARED!!!

###

'ARMADILLO ON THE HALF SHELL'

Armadillo on the half shell

　　baking in the sun,

why didn't you pay attention

　　when your momma said to run??

The highway is a treacherous place

　　for little creatures, such as you!

If you'd just been a little faster

　　...you wouldn't be 'Roadkill Stew'!

Armadillo on the half shell

　　baking in the sun,

you still look medium rare

　　but Mister Buzzard says

　　　...'You're DONE!!'

###

'HILARIOUS MOON AND THE DAUGHTERS OF DOOM'

(Dedicated to all who were bullied)

Hilarious Moon was a dancer

    with hair the color of flame.

Her face was lit with sunshine,

    with a smile that matched her name.

Her arms and legs were skinny,

    she danced to a different beat.

The music playing in her head

    had her dancing in the street!

She was her Daddy's beauty,

    had her Momma's eyes and chin,

but when she met some girls at school

    ...Hilarious couldn't win.

So excited for the third grade...

      Hilarious loved her school and room.

Everyone was getting along

      until the arrival of the 'Daughters of Doom'!

"Green Cowboy boots are ugly!!"

      "We don't like your purple plaid!"

"Your tights are striped and yellow!"

      "Your whole sense of style is bad!!!"

"WHY IS YOUR NAME SO STUPID??"

      "WHY IS YOUR HAIR SO RED???"

The 'Daughters of Doom' were frowning;

      this is what Hilarious said.

"I got my hair from my Grandma

      ...she wore it wild and free!"

"My parents wanted a special name

that would only be for me!"

"They didn't want a usual name,

It had to be fitting and fun!"

"As soon as they saw their baby girl

· ...they knew they picked the right one!!"

"My Mom said just to be myself

...be whatever I want to be."

"My name is just 'Hilarious'

...and I only want to be me!!"

"Why do you girls have to be so mean??

Hilarious, don't you hide!"

Welcome support came from Bobby George

who had stepped to Hilarious' side.

"Why can't we all just get along?

   Everyone isn't the same!

I'm big-boned, just like my Dad

   ...and I like Hilarious' name!"

Then, Darcy Dang stepped forward.

   "You girls bullied me, too!

You said there's something wrong with me

   ...but there's something wrong with you!!"

"You're right; I have to wear braces,

   but Mom says that's only now.

I'm growing into my beauty,

   we all change...that's how!!"

Harlan Rhodes had trouble reading,

   Joey Briggs was in a wheelchair.

Even though they were learning and trying

...the 'Daughters of Doom' didn't care.

When her classmates saw her bullied

...they stepped up and took a stand.

They took the chance to be helpful

...and gave Hilarious a hand!

As more kids stood beside her,

and support for Hilarious increased,

the 'Daughters of Doom' backed away

...and their bullying...ceased!!

###

'BROTHERS'

We are brothers, we're friends...we've been arch enemies!

We've wrestled and fought...and bloodied our knees.

We've played cowboys and Indians...built forts in the snow.

We skipped rocks on the river...and learned how to throw.

We discovered dinosaurs...we raced on our trikes.

We played trucks and cars...till Santa brought bikes!

We caught tadpoles and frogs, caught fish and one snake!

Dad taught us to swim and to ski at the lake.

We burned s'mores in a campfire...told ghost stories all night,

Then we huddled together...until the first light.

We played baseball and football, dunked a hoop or two.

We discovered girls. We discovered beer, too!

We grew and got older...now grown into men.

I love you, my brother...I love you, my friend.

###

'FOREVER FRIENDS'

We'll always be 'Forever Friends',

    this I know is true.

We'll stick together through thick and thin

    ...and always love each other, too.

We survived a Tennessee tornado,

    drank lime daiquiris, chilled and fine!

We road tripped with the top down

    ...and jumped a deer on 99!!

We've gorged ourselves on ice cream.

    We (you) 'mooned' one crazy night.

We cried together when things went wrong,

    We've cried when things went right!

We've gathered on the holidays

　　...the seasons pass so fast.

We've celebrated birthdays

　　...and the years went whizzing past.

Through weddings, births, and funerals,

　　through endings and broken hearts,

Through triumphs, wrecks, and tragedies

　　...through beginnings and new starts.

Our friendship remains a constant

　　as our families have grown.

We are the sisters we chose ourselves

　　...you're the best friend I've ever known.

　　###

'IRISH ANGEL'

I'm sending this Irish Angel

from Heavenly skies of blue,

To bring these best of wishes

...especially to you.

I wish you Love within your heart

...and warmth within your Home.

I wish for you, safe travels

...wherever you may roam.

Wishing Health, Wealth, and Happiness

to last you through the years.

I wish you Friends and Laughter

...and only Joyous tears.

###

'BOATERS'

Some dream of being sailors

    ...living life upon the Sea.

If that's your heart's true vision

    ...I hope it comes to be.

A boat, by definition

    before you cast off on the Blue,

It's a hole in water surrounded by wood

    that you throw your money into!

A sailor's life can be romantic,

    but often... that's not his lot.

Especially if he's unprepared,

    he'll get his shorts up in a knot!!

Remember to always watch the tides

    ...heed warnings of any storm!

Don't moor too closely to rocky reefs

    ...the water isn't warm!

Keep the ballast on the bottom

    and the sails upon the top,

then head for the nearest alee port

    If the barometer should drop!

If giant waves are battering

    making it hard to stay afloat,

and you notice fins are circling

    ...IT'S TIME FOR A BIGGER BOAT!!!

Enjoy your 'high seas' adventures

    ...I'm sorry I'm such a slouch.

I'm going to watch the 'PERFECT STORM'

    from the safety of my couch!

###

'AN EAGLE FLEW AWAY'

(In memory of OSP Trooper Jody Dye;

Killed in the Line of Duty on July 5, 1985)

The Troopers marched in cadence

        Carrying a comrade in his sleep,

their faces carved of granite, their emotions hard to keep.

Cruisers passed in silence with beacons flashing bright,

To honor with the procession...a life that lost the fight.

Crowds stood along the roadway,

        some bowed their heads in prayer.

They held the respectful vigil,

        they wanted to show they care.

With gun salutes and plaintive Taps

        we buried a man in Grey.

        A stallion pranced by riderless

        ...and an Eagle flew away.

###

'A LITTLE INSANITY'

Boil a cauldron of this elixir

    ...and drink this insanity brew.

When I saw it sitting on the shelf

    ...I immediately thought of you!

Insanity is contagious.

    We catch it from our kids!

Sometimes we're catatonic

    ...sometimes we flip our lids!!

So, have a cup of insanity

    to start out every day.

The best defense is a swift offense

    ...so strike first in every way!

A little insanity's a good thing,

    It keeps most trouble away!

No one messes with a lunatic

...YOU'LL BE SAFE OUTSIDE THE FRAY!!!

So raise a cup of mania

if you think you have the guts.

A little insanity's healthy

...it keeps up from going NUTS!

Enhance your personal neurosis

with a 'cup of crazy' brew,

And embrace a little insanity

...I'm right there with you, too!!!

###

' BAD TIMES '

We all have gone through bad times;

    unfortunate...but it's true.

Sometimes...you get that bull!

    Sometimes...that old bull gets you!

Though we work so hard, and struggle

    trying our best to not get hurt;

sometimes that bull just hooks us

    ...and throws us in the dirt!!!

Every Cowboy has a bad day

    and gets bucked off upside down;

but his simple prayers are answered

    ...when he's rescued by a Clown!

When the storm is all around us

    and the rain is in our eyes,

We'll pray for winds to push the clouds

...and bring us bluer skies.

So, we get up, dust off, try harder;

giving it all our best.

We'll persevere through blood and tears

...it's what separates us from the rest!

So, if things get far beyond you;

remember family...and your friends!

We'll make it through, together.

We'll all triumph in the end!

In those darkest hours

when mistakes are all we make,

Remember; when that bullfight's over

...we'll all be eating STEAK!!

###

'SNOWBIRDS'

When winter falls on the northland
bringing ice and drifting snow,
the Snowbird migration starts southward
...sunny Florida is where they go!

Behold...the mighty Snowbirds
flocking south on 95,
driving RV's the size of Kansas
...keeping southern commerce alive!!

Drakes are greatly empowered
wearing shirts that are flowered
as they golf for the ultimate prize.
They'll snorkel the Keys
...swim with manatees
...and eat cheeseburgers in Paradise!

Snow hens will bake and broil in coconut oil

till their pale, northern skins tan to leather.

They'll drink sweet tea and drawl

      calling everyone...y'all

    while enjoying the tropical weather!

They'll bike and surf; they'll walk on the beach

      ...maybe skinny dip in the pool.

They'll visit the mouse in his turreted house

      ...because in Florida, it's a rule!

But when summer is near and temperatures sear

    the northbound migration begins.

They'll head for the cold leaving Yankee gold

    and hopefully next year...

      they'll bring friends!!

      ###

'THE CRYSTAL BALLROOM'

On Buckeye Lake in summertime

    when nights are soft and still;

remember a time not long ago

    and imagine...if you will.

Close your eyes and dance again

    across the Crystal Ballroom floor.

Hold your lover cheek to cheek

    to the music played long before.

Listen to your memories

    and hear Dorsey's sweet refrain.

Trot to Les Brown's 'Band of Renown'

when they fire up that 'Chattanooga Train'.

Hear Goodman, White, and Ellington

    play old standards through the night,

then swing to the Glenn Miller Orchestra

    under whirling, crystal light.

Even now, at Buckeye Lake

when dark replaces day,

if you listen very carefully

...you can still hear the music play.

##

'BUCKEYE LAKE'

The misted morning shrouds the dawn

in shades of deepest pink.

With Herons' cries

to scarlet skies

over water... black as ink.

The moon falls away to another day

leaving heavens of azure hue.

A lost breeze sings

through white Geese wings

and their feathers turn to blue.

Then yellow fingers streak the sky

and boats strain at the stake.

The light has come,

a new day begun

on beautiful Buckeye Lake.

But when the sunshine wearies,

deep purple claims the light.

A blue Goose wings

while a Heron sings

as they fly into the night.

###

'YOU ARE LOVED'

Wherever you may wander, wherever you may go,

There is one simple thing I want you to know:

You are loved in the mountains,

You are loved on the Plains.

You are loved in the sunshine

...you are loved when it rains.

You are loved in the Moonlight

With stars in your eyes,

You are loved in 'Hellos'

...you are loved through 'Goodbyes'.

You are loved when you're angry,

You are loved when you're mad!

You are loved in the good times

...and you're loved in the bad.

You are loved through the Seasons

...through a lifetime, you see.

If you haven't guessed

...you are loved by me.

(To Matt and Brandi, Erin and Brad; our grandchildren; Makenna, Dylan, Conner, and Lily, and our new great-granddaughter; Leighton Grace)

'THE HOLLOW'

Listen to the joyful songs

    Of the Meadowlark and the Wren,

as they celebrate their voices

    in this shady, Kansas glen.

Lovers stroll down limestone steps

    toward the cavern and the stream.

The gazebo perches gracefully

    sheltering those who come to dream.

A crystal wonderland in Winter,

    Chautauqua prairie winds will bring

promises of sultry Summer nights

    ...and Redbuds in the Spring.

A Bullfrog lends his baritone

    to the Whippoorwill and the Swallow,

singing in memory of those beautiful Spirits

    who left their Souls in Sedan's Hollow.

###

'THE FIRETRUCK'

When I was just a young child

     and daydreams filled my head,

I'd dream of being a Fireman

     on a Firetruck...all shiny and red!

Then one year at Christmastime

     when I crept down to our tree;

there under twinkling holiday lights

     was the most beautiful sight to see.

A regal truck of scarlet

     stood sparkling, bright and new;

reflected in the moonlight

     throwing lasers of crimson hue!

I sat in awe outside the light

     watching reddened prisms play

across the floor and up the walls

     until night was turned to day.

In those magic moments

of the quiet and the still;

my heart beat as a Fireman's heart

...I know it always will.

But when my life is over

and I finally lay my head;

Lord, carry me up to Heaven

on a Firetruck... all shiny and red.

###

'FISH TALES'

It seems to me some Fishermen

       Have a problem with length and size!

Not saying their calculations are wrong

       ...but I fear THEY MIGHT BE LIES!!

Their fish tales are embellished

       with minnows turned to whales!

Until the weekend weigh-in

       with the truth told by the scales!

I've studied the best chefs' secrets

       to prepare a gourmet dish.

I've baked, and broiled, and fried them

       ...but they still always smell like fish!!

We all have hooked a monster...

       though yours wasn't as big as mine!

I'd have the proof to show you

       ...but the damned thing broke my line!!

Photos always tell the truth

       Or so I've heard it said.

So, don't look at my albums

       Until I'm long past dead!!

When my fishing days are over

       this will be my final wish;

Lord, please carry me up to Heaven,

       near a good spot...WHERE I CAN FISH!!!!

       ###

'GRAMPA'

You once were a young blade with abs of steel!

You had thick, wavy hair...your knees were real!

You loved with abandon, made touchdowns galore.

You played in a band...your prowess was LORE!!

Your skin was unblemished, nary a freckle or fold,

your belly was flat...your beer always cold!

You danced the 'Twist' at all the school hops,

you drag-raced your friends and ran from the Cops!!!

Now things have changed, you have insidious gas!

Your hair disappeared; you keep your teeth in a glass!

Your brow was unwrinkled, now clenched in a frown

'cause what used to go up...now sadly points down!!

You've learned the true meaning of the term;

'Golden Years'.

Your gold goes to doctors who confirm your worst fears!!

So, give it a go...try to pee and not miss!

Then go raise your glass

...and give your Grandchildren a kiss!!

###

'I AM A SOLDIER'

I am a Soldier...and Proud I'll always be

to Protect and Serve the U.S.A., she is safe because of me.

Salute 'Old Glory' proudly

    as she waves Red, White, and Blue!

Pledge allegiance from your heart.

    That is all I ask of you.

September 11th taught us our future is at war

    with those who 'woke the Tiger';

        now America sleeps no more.

If I am sent to battle to lands across the sea,

    send each day your loving prayers

        as I fight for Liberty.

I am a Soldier...and Proud I'll always be.

    Welcome me home with open arms

        ...you are safe because of me.

    ###

'PRAYER FOR VICTIMS'

Grant strength to all victims

who lie awake in fear.

Give them peace of heart and courage

...and let them know we're here.

When solitude surrounds them

and they face demons in the night,

please help us to understand,

and comfort them in their fight.

For those who lost the battle

...we'll say a silent prayer.

Please tell them that we love them,

and let them know...we care.

(Rest in peace, Lionel)

'SMYRNA SERENADE'

Come to New Smyrna,

    waltz upon this land,

        created by Neptune's pearls

            ... crushed to alabaster sand.

Spread your wings with Seagulls,

    Soar on the ocean breeze.

        Dive with Rays and Dolphins

            ...ballet with Manatees!

Close your eyes and take a breath

    Of Smyrna's fresh salt air,

        commingled with scents of jasmine

            and blooms of hibiscus, there!

Crabwalk with dancing Sandpipers

    performing the Pelican promenade.

        Let the surf's soul rhythm lull you

            with the Smyrna Serenade!

Listen to your heartbeat

matching breakers on the shore,

and know you'll always love her

...New Smyrna, forevermore.

###

'REMEMBERING HARLEY ™'

Remember what your youth was like

    when you threw caution to the wind,

jumping as high as your legs could throw

    then falling to Earth, again?

Remember running into the breeze

    Coaxing a hesitant kite;

feeling the thrill when it tugged the line

    and joyfully took flight?

I remember the day I heard the growl

    of a Harley ™ on the street.

Watched it pass all chrome and gleam

    ...and knew our paths would meet.

Now, a Harley™ owns me

to ride with my life through,

exploring far horizons

under painted skies of blue.

As I fly on the back of my cycle,

Summer winds blow jealously.

Now, I'm the kite that tugs the line

...life has been good to me.

The power of this Harley™

Is like a love you can't control!

Some people say "It's just a bike."

I say..."It's just my soul!"

###

'SISTERS'

We are sisters, we're friends,

    we were Daddy's little girls.

We were tumblers and tomboys

    ...and princesses in curls!

We were ballerinas in tutus...

    we could sing a 'High C'.

We were fearless explorers

    ...and mermaids of the sea.

We had tea parties...and dolls,

    we drank cherry Kool-Aid™.

We played dress-up with lipstick

    and ate cookies Mom made!

We shared dreams and puppies

    ...went to the same schools.

We gossiped about boys

    ...and giggled like fools!

Childhood was fleeting;

  but our memories last.

Though we've grown into women

  ...we still smile at the past.

We've danced like banshees,

  had boyfriends, galore.

We've walked up the aisle

  ...we've kicked some to the door.

We've rocked our babies,

  stood together when sad,

We are each other's confidants

  ...we buried Mom and Dad.

By remembering the good times

  ...they will never end.

I love you, my sister,

  I love you, my friend.

  ###

'THIS MAN'

This man of passions bright and passions bold

Does rend my heart and tear at me

...but satisfies all dreams to be.

So, cast your fate to blinded sight

Evoke emotions of the night!

Laugh with this man of reckless heart.

Dance in dreams of bliss!

Burn in the fire of his passion,

and drown in the depth of his kiss!

But rise no further than you can fall

...measure love...don't give it all.

For this man of passions bright and passions bold

...he is to have

...but not to hold.

###

'I DON'T KNOW HOW TO FEEL'

I can't believe you did this,

Can't believe it's real.

I love you...and I hate you,

I just don't know how to feel.

What went on in your mind?

Why couldn't you confide?

Why didn't you tell me

you were thinking of suicide?

What burning drive within your brain

made you want to cut short your years?

Was it the sudden ending

of many hidden fears?

I can't believe you did this,

Can't believe it's real.

I love you...and I hate you!

I just don't know how to feel.

Why did you do this, Darlin'?

Was it for some welcome relief?

Or just to cause the rest of us

a never-ending, revenging grief?

This act was cruel and selfish.

You threw away our dreams!

Did you suddenly stop loving me

because that is how it seems?

I'm angry...and I'm bitter;

was it me...or was it you?

I cry, but I can't find the tears

though my heart is ripped in two!

Now, no one will ever know

...never find out why

or what possessed you Darlin'

...to want to die.

I can't believe you did this.

Can't believe it's real.

I love you...and I hate you.

I don't know how to feel.

I love you...and I hate you.

I just don't know how to feel.

###

'MEMORIES'

Tears flow gently

    ...seeping...prying,

Into the pillow

    ...wet with crying.

Stifled and smothered

    ...discovery defies,

Shed in the memory

    of final goodbyes.

    ###

'THE SEEMING SADNESS'

The seeming sadness of the trees,

   of the songs sung through the leaves

Is multiplied by tears

   ...and voice of memories.

The seeming sadness does decree

   of the life that will not be,

again comes hope of love

   ...and life returns to me.

###

'PARTNERS'

We are Partners, this majestic Dog and I.

We'll patrol the streets for days to come

as we have in nights gone by.

A gentle beast with family, but criminals; BEWARE!

He's the very teeth within the Law;

to him, swift justice is fair.

No lies will pass between us; he's all things I strive to be.

Strong...brave...and loyal;

he'd lay down his life for me.

He knows my soul and I love his, together, till the end.

. He's more than just my Partner

...he'll always be my friend.

When our final watch is over

and the time has come to part,

I'll forever have him with me

...his pawprint is on my heart.

###

'THE ROSE'

He gave to me, a rose

and vows on breezes borne.

The wind dispersed his promises;

my blood is on the thorn.

###

'WAITING'

Leaning over the wooden bridge

    skirting a grassy glade,

waiting for her lover

    ...stands a fair, young maid.

Gazing into the limpid pond

    for the final inspection;

slowly turning sadly away

    ...for it's an old face in the reflection.

###

'WHO?'

Always, I try to avoid it,

    away from its path to steer,

but always it finds and haunts me

    ...the flirtatious ghost of fear.

Flirting within...without,

    through and under my skin,

fearing the loss of loved ones

    ...for who will love me, then?

###

'SUDDENLY'

Suddenly: Born

              Life

              Morn

Suddenly: Talking

              Crawling

              Walking

Suddenly: Running

              Playing

              Cunning

Suddenly: Dating

              Loving

              Mating

Suddenly: Grown

              Old

              Known

Suddenly: Crying

              Remembering

              Dying

###

'LADY LIBERTY CRIED'

We stood in the Valley of the Shadow of Death

and stared in disbelief,

at this place of indescribable horror

and unimaginable grief.

We've memorized faces of victims

who came from our cities and farms.

We tried our best to help them

...and embraced them in our arms.

We listened as everyday heroes

wrestled Flight 93 to the ground.

We heard their rally cry..."LET'S ROLL!!"

...then heard that one, last, awful sound.

We watched our Police and Firemen

as they sacrificed their lives;

and when Flight 77 hit the Pentagon

...we listened to their cries.

We've seen tears and lives forever changed

...we'll never be the same.

But we will prevail with strength of heart

...America is our name.

From the dust and mangled steel

where America was on her knees;

we watched her rise and raise our Flag

...and we saw 'Old Glory' swell the breeze.

September 11th, 2001;

the morning that thousands died.

We watched the Towers come tumbling down

...and Lady Liberty cried.

Jenny Keeley, Sept. 2001
NOVA Team One

###

*In Memory of all victims and their families of the
attacks of 9/11, and to all First Responders... with Love.